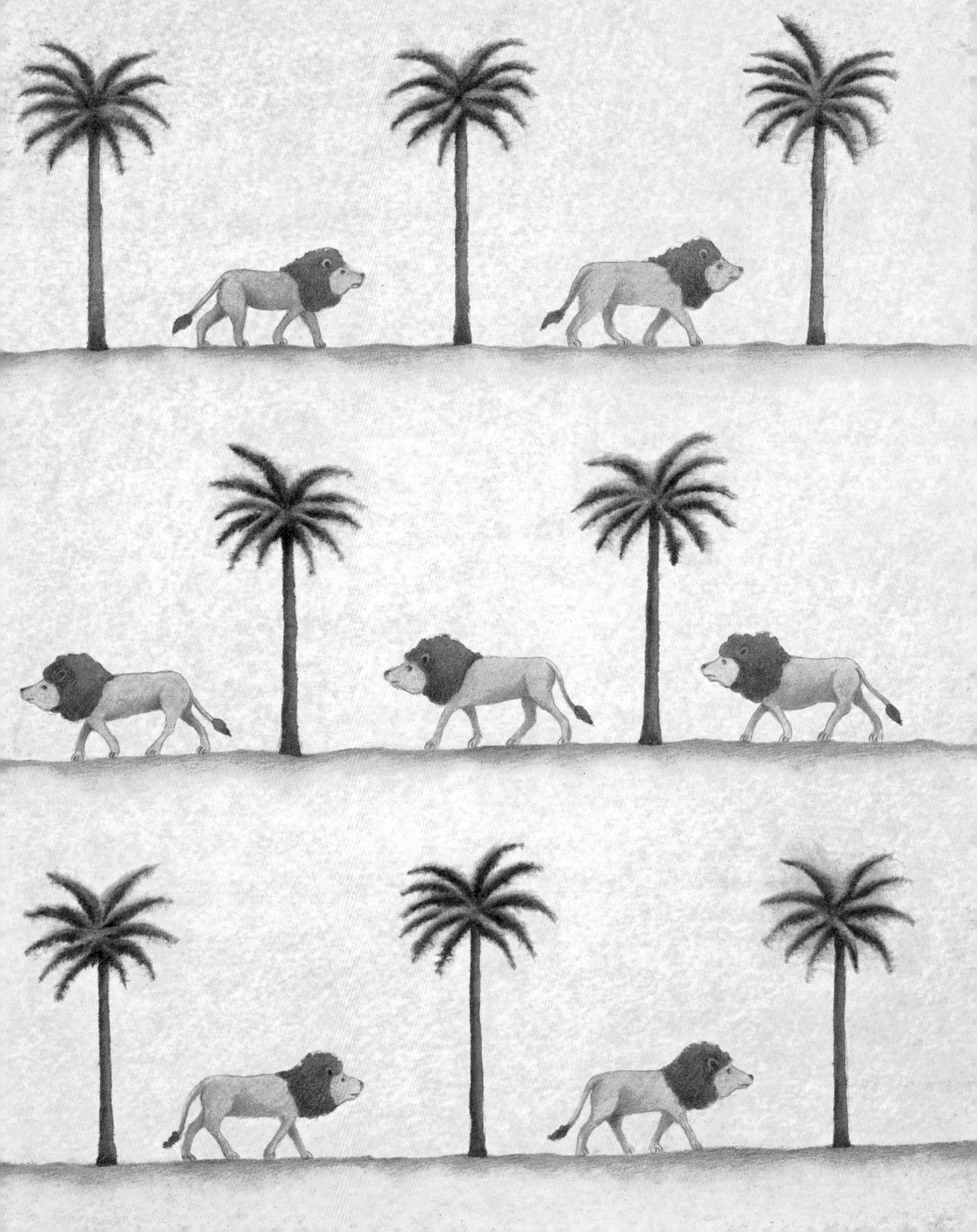

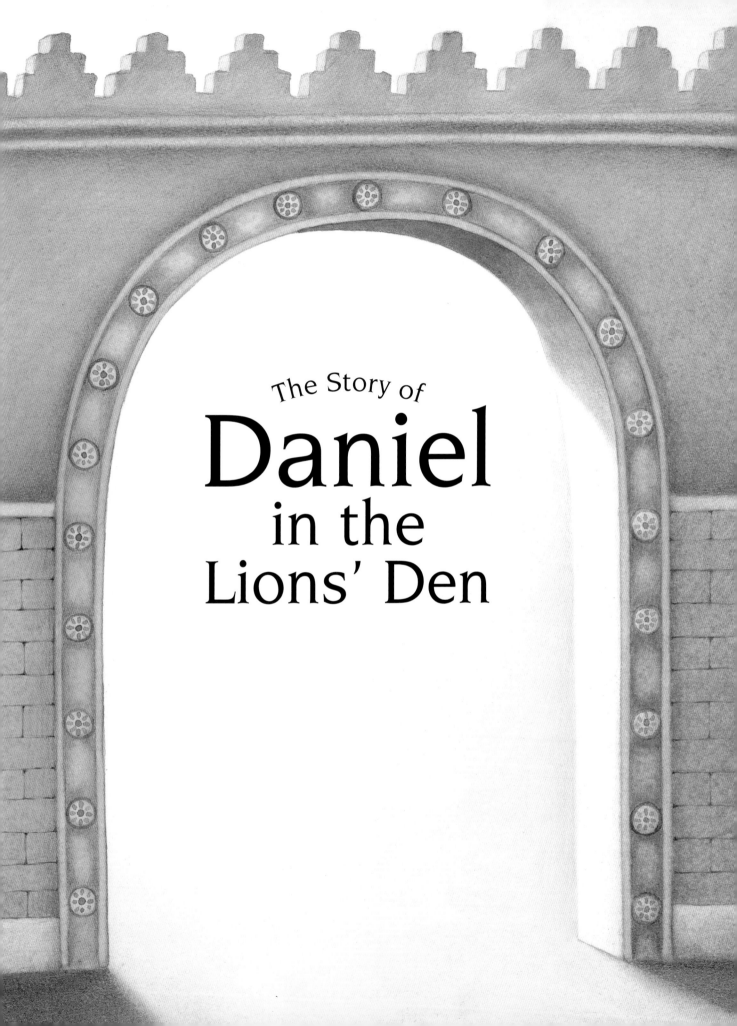

The Story of
Daniel
in the
Lions' Den

To my great nieces and nephews: Alexandrea and Aaron, Daniel, Darragh, and Orla — M. McC.

To my friend, Luca — G. F.

Barefoot Books
3 Bow Street, 3rd Floor
Cambridge, MA 02138

Text copyright © 2003 by Michael McCarthy
Illustrations copyright © 2003 by Giuliano Ferri
The moral right of Michael McCarthy to be identified as the author and Giuliano Ferri
to be identified as the illustrator of this work has been asserted

This book was typeset in Novarese Medium 18pt on 26pt leading
The illustrations were prepared in watercolors and
colored pencils on watercolor paper
Graphic design by designsection, Frome
Color separation by Bright Art Graphics, Singapore
Printed and bound in Singapore by Tien Wah Press (Pte) Ltd

This book has been printed on 100% acid-free paper

ISBN 1 84148 209 9

135798642

Publisher Cataloging-in-Publication Data (U.S.)

McCarthy, Michael.
    The story of Daniel in the lions' den / retold by Michael McCarthy;
illustrated by Giuliano Ferri._1st ed.
[32] p. : col. ill. ; cm.
Summary: Retells the Old Testament story in which Daniel,
imprisoned in a den of hungry lions as a punishment for praying to God,
is protected by an angel.
ISBN 1-84148-209-9
1. Daniel (Biblical character)—Juvenile literature.
2. Bible. O.T.—Legends—Juvenile literature.
I. Ferri, Giuliano. II. Daniel in the lions' den. III. Title.

224/.509505 21   2003

The Story of
Daniel
in the
Lions' Den

retold by Michael McCarthy

illustrated by Giuliano Ferri

Barefoot Books
Celebrating Art and Story

Daniel was scared when soldiers came
To plunder his home in Jerusalem.
And when their cruel work was done
They took him away to Babylon.

There the king, Nabuchadnezzar,
Saw that Daniel was very clever.
So he was welcomed to the court
To learn the language, culture, sport.

Daniel was thankful that he was safe,
But he never forgot his childhood faith.
Three times each day he stopped and prayed.
It helped him to feel less afraid.

One night, the king had a scary dream.
He woke in a sweat and began to scream.
None of his sages could help him out;
Only Daniel could tell what the dream was about.

The king was grateful; and so, in stages,
He put Daniel in charge of the royal sages.
And because he could find no person wiser
Daniel became his chief advisor.

A long time passed; the good king died,
Daniel still serving at his side.
Everyone mourned Nabuchadnezzar.
Next came his son, King Belshazzar.

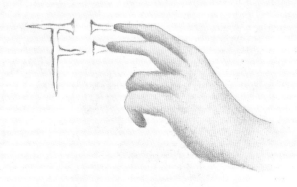

Belshazzar gave his friends a party.
They ate too much and drank too hearty.
When late at night, before them all,
A hand appeared upon the wall.

The king gasped. It was very frightening.
No one there could read the writing.
Then Daniel, with the king's consent,
Told them what the message meant.

"The king," he said, "won't reign much longer.
His crown will fall to someone stronger."
And sure enough, that very night,
King Belshazzar was put to flight.

A horde of Medes and Persians came,
Darius was the new king's name.
He called together his advisors
To choose some local supervisors.

Daniel was honest, wise and fair.
He worked with vigor, verve and flair.
King Darius was most impressed;
He chose him over all the rest.

The other men were very jealous.
"We'll not have this-here Daniel tell us
What to do!" So they began
To hatch a low and wicked plan.

The king should pass a proclamation
Outlawing prayer across the nation.
Then all the people would give praise
To him alone for thirty days.

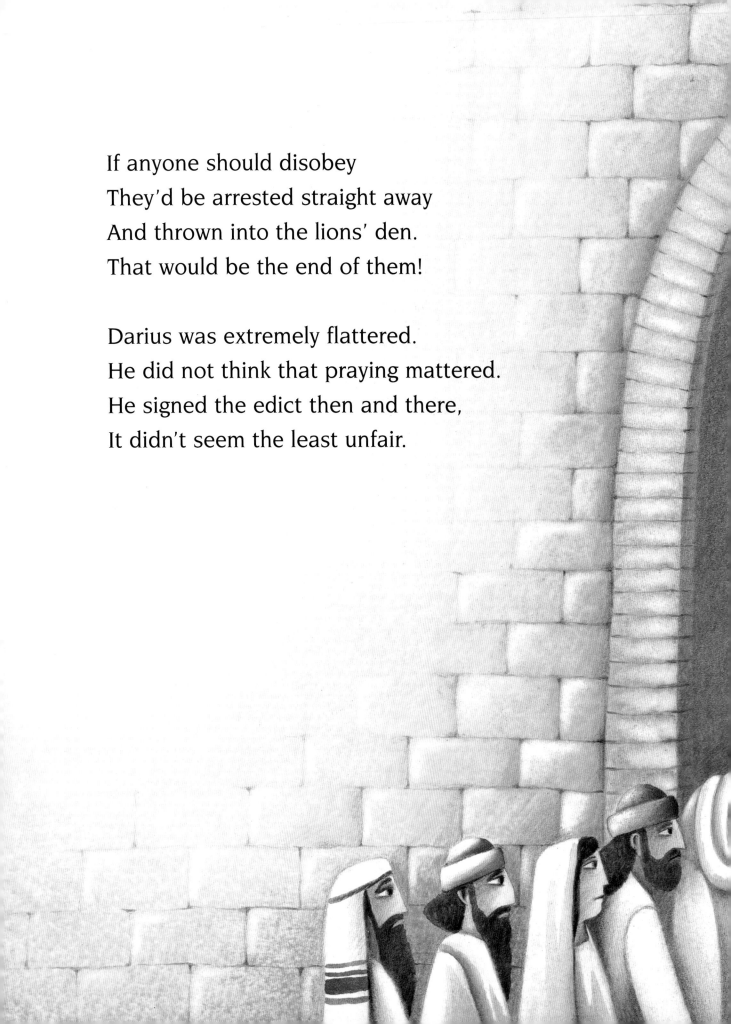

If anyone should disobey
They'd be arrested straight away
And thrown into the lions' den.
That would be the end of them!

Darius was extremely flattered.
He did not think that praying mattered.
He signed the edict then and there,
It didn't seem the least unfair.

Now, Daniel still prayed every day.
This had always been his way.
The plotters spied him with no trouble.
"We've got him now — we'll burst his bubble!"

They called Darius out with glee,
Spreading their hands and saying, "See!"
Too late he recognized the plot —
He was already hooked and caught.

Darius was angry and alarmed;
For he did not want Daniel harmed.
But once the edict had been signed
He could no longer change his mind.

Daniel was taken down the steps
To where the pride of lions slept.
The soldiers left him there alone,
And blocked the entrance with a stone.

Soon the lions were on their feet.
It was long past their time to eat.
When Daniel stepped into the pit
The lions thought, "Mmm! This is it!"

The chief of lions had the right
To take the first delicious bite.
His mane stood up, so big and hairy,
His eyes were bright, his jaws were scary.

His shoulders were both broad and strong;
His back was wide and lean and long.
He was a wild and rugged beast,
And he was ready for a feast.

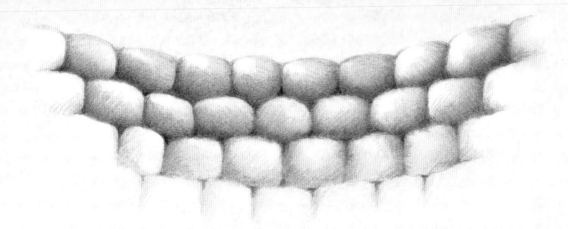

But Daniel was quite free from fear
Because he knew that God was near.
He stood there tall, prepared to die,
And looked that lion in the eye.

The lion looked Daniel up and down,
His face wore a bewildered frown.
He stared about him, searching, gazing.
He found the whole thing quite amazing.

The pride had not seen this before!
They waited for their master's roar.
It never came. The reason's clear:
A lion only roars at fear.

At last, the lion dropped his glare.
He pawed the ground and sniffed the air.
He shook his head, gave one long yawn,
And settled down to sleep 'til dawn.

The other lions did the same,
Lying down there, still and tame.
Daniel knelt and prayed awhile,
Thanking God with a quiet smile.

And slowly, as the night grew colder,
He lay against the lion's shoulder.
Then gave a sigh and, breathing deep,
Snuggled up and went to sleep.

But Darius did not sleep a wink.
He was so upset he couldn't think.
When morning came, he called his men
And hastened to the lions' den.

He called out loud in fear and dread:
"Daniel, are you there?" he said.
Daniel called back, loud and clear,
"God has saved me. I am here!"

The king, of course, was overjoyed.
The plotters' plan had been destroyed.
The soldiers moved the stone away,
And there was Daniel — hip, hurray!

"The lions are starving," Darius said.
"Now let them eat these rogues instead."
And that was how those wicked wretches
Were punished for their schemes and sketches.

And here is how the story ended.
The edict was at once suspended.
Instead, wherever people prayed
Daniel's God would be obeyed.

The king himself sent out the order
To all the land from sea to border.
It spread as quickly as a flame
And all the people praised God's name.

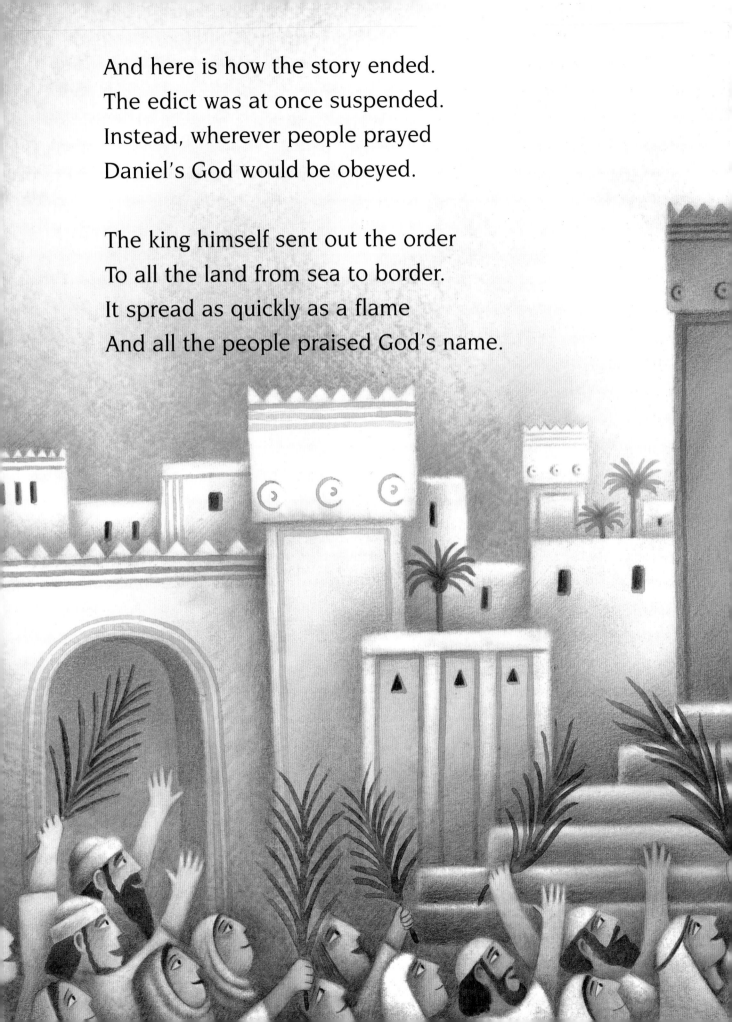

Author's Note

The story of Daniel's life is an interesting one, and it was a challenge to present it in a way that would be accessible to young readers. I started by reading many translations, mainly the New Jerusalem Bible, and the New Revised Standard Version. Then I studied Biblical commentaries, especially the Jerome Biblical Commentary, to understand the context of the story, and the purpose behind its telling.

The story of Daniel originates from the 6th century B.C. The historical basis of the narrative is less important than the moral message it carries — its main purpose was to encourage Jews to remain faithful to their religion at a time when the allure of the surrounding pagan culture was strong. The author was concerned with demonstrating the superiority of Israel's God over the merely human wisdom of the pagans, and to show how God's power triumphed over their persecutors.

After this phase of research, I wrote a prose synopsis of this very complex tale, rich in mythology and dreams. My aim was to condense the material without losing any of the layers of richness and meaning. As I worked on the text, I remembered how I was terrified of dogs as a child. Being frightened seemed to draw their attention to me all the more. When I eventually overcame my fears, they seemed to lose all interest in me. So I wondered if Daniel's lack of fear, because God's Angel was with him, was a factor in the lions lying down to sleep. This was a breakthrough point in the writing of the story.

Finally, with a condensed prose version, I set off for a week to Egypt. During this time I visited the Biblical sites of Mount Sinai. The rhythm of the verses began to come to me and the first verse draft was complete before my return. I tested it in my local primary school in Yorkshire, England. The children's responses and reactions helped me edit and polish and hone until the final product emerged. I hope that the story of Daniel, as I have told it here, will be a source of joy and learning for children for a long time to come.

Michael McCarthy

Barefoot Books
Celebrating Art and Story

At Barefoot Books, we celebrate art and story with books that open
the hearts and minds of children from all walks of life, inspiring them to read
deeper, search further, and explore their own creative gifts. Taking our
inspiration from many different cultures, we focus on themes that encourage
independence of spirit, enthusiasm for learning, and acceptance of other
traditions. Thoughtfully prepared by writers, artists and storytellers from
all over the world, our products combine the best of the present with the best
of the past to educate our children as the caretakers of tomorrow.

www.barefootbooks.com